CANADIAN WINGS

THE PASSION AND THE FORCE

To my father, Jack, and to the memory of my mother, Mary.

First published in 1990 by
McGraw-Hill Ryerson Limited
330 Progress Avenue
Scarborough, Ontario M1P 2Z5

Produced for McGraw-Hill Ryerson Limited
by Image House, Ottawa, Canada

Editors: Nancy Huggett, Andrea Gallagher Ellis
Photo Lab Services: Techniphoto Ltd. Ottawa
Production: Aerographics, Ottawa
Typesetting: David Berman TypoGraphics, Ottawa

Canadian Cataloguing in Publication Data

McQuarrie, John,
Canadian wings

1. Canada. Canadian Armed Forces. Air Command.
2. Aeronautics, Military – Canada. 3. Air pilots,
Military – Canada. I. Title.

UG635.C3M26   1990   358.4'00971   C90-093758-0

ISBN 0-07-551010-3

Printed and bound in Singapore

C A N A D I A N
WINGS
T H E   P A S S I O N   A N D   T H E   F O R C E

TEXT AND PHOTOS: **JOHN MCQUARRIE**   DESIGN: **DAVID O'MALLEY**

FOREWORD

Beauty is in the eye of the beholder. After a 35-year love affair with military aviation and 16 years of operational flying, I was moved by the beauty of the photographs that grace this book. Against the magnificent backdrop of Canada and the diverse areas of the world where our Canadian Air Force operates, readers are treated to a feast of images and text. Together they tell a fascinating story of a peacetime air force poised for operational duties anywhere in the world as required by the Government of Canada.

John McQuarrie's photographs tell not only a graphic story of Canada's Air Force today but capture the mood that has prevailed for decades: Canadians are born to fly, aviation is in our blood.

This book focuses on military aviation. Young men and women, cadets and not-so-young men and women tell their story, a familiar one reflecting pride of service and self-achievement.

From operations in the Sinai to sovereignty missions, the men and women who comprise Canada's Air Force today reflect the courage and character of those who preceded them. They are no less important. A nation such as Canada with huge land, sea and airspaces, with alliance commitments and international responsibilities for peace-keeping and international aid, depends heavily on a young, innovative and well-equipped air force. This tradition continues. John McQuarrie's photographs are the proof.

Lieutenant General Larry A. Ashley
CMM, CD, CF (Ret'd)
President, Lockheed Canada Inc.

INTRODUCTION

As the dream of this book turned the corner from imagination to reality it was decided that you, the reader, would have 160 pages. As your photographer and scribe I was concerned that I would have to stretch to fulfil this requirement. It didn't turn out that way! We forced ourselves to stop at 200 pages and there were many more good ones we would love to have given you.

But don't blame me. There are about 30,000 men and women serving in the Canadian Air Force. During the last year I had the great pleasure and privilege to share fragments of many of these fine peoples' lives. Their generosity and cheerful tolerance of this civilian led directly to the words and images you will experience within these pages. It is they who must bear the responsibility for the pages you will not see, for it was they who provided such a wealth of material, both words and images, that the problem became one of editing down rather than filling in. A good problem to have!

There are very few captions accompanying the images herein. Similarly, there are no names and no specific squadron references. This is intended to be a visual experience complemented by personal descriptions and feelings, candidly expressed, by members of the Air Force. Fabric and texture in the vernacular.

If you have an appetite for fact and detail I refer you to the undisputed master historian and chronicler of Canadian military aviation, Larry Milberry. In *Canada's Air Force Today* and *Sixty Years: The RCAF and CF Air Command 1924-1984*, Mr. Milberry provides the most complete, factual account imaginable of the Air Force past and present. If you want to know who did what, with what and where, and if you like photographs of airplanes, you will find it all in these two fine books.

In an age of relative peace and prosperity there will always be questions about the wisdom of directing a large portion of the national treasure to defence. Well-meaning men and women in government have the difficult task of directing ever scarcer resources to the most appropriate places and this has resulted in sometimes controversial cuts in defence spending. In the military it has meant that fewer people have fewer resources to accomplish their tasks. These budget constraints, coupled with higher salaries in all fields of the booming commercial aviation world, have caused a number of good people to leave the Air Force, but this problem is currently being addressed.

The Air Force and this country can be grateful, however, that we continue to retain a large percentage of experienced people, just as the recruiters continue to attract the best of our younger generation. Of the thousand or more Air Force men and women I met, there was not one I would be less than delighted to have as neighbour or friend.

And so, to all the members of the Air Force who placed your faith in me to give an honest portrayal, I sincerely hope my vision of you is worthy of that trust. My only regret is that, with the publication of this book, my great adventure with you is over.

John McQuarrie

ACKNOWLEDGMENTS

The spirited individuals who contributed to making this book just a little bit better than it would have been without their help, are named on this page. While I made a concerted effort to record all your names I know I will have missed a few. If I photographed you or talked with you about your job, if you drove or flew me somewhere, I hope you will find your name here because your cheerful assistance is reflected in the pages that follow. If I missed you I am truly sorry and I hope you will make it a point to rag me over my lapse at the earliest opportunity.

John Aiken
MCpl Andy Ainslie
Capt J.R. Alarie
Capt Mark Albers
Capt Elizabeth Allan
Capt "Vic" Anciaux (Belgian AF)
Maj Brent Anderson
Capt Jim "Andy" Anderson
Capt Allan Andrukow
Jacques Anka
Maj Rick Anscomb
Cpl Denis Antille
Capt Shane Antaya
Pte Todd Argentino
Maj Roger Arsenault
Sgt Atkinson
Sgt Rob Ashwood
Cpl Pete Awender
LCol John "Chief" Bagshaw
MCpl Chris Baillile-David
Capt Pat Baisley
MCpl John Baker
MCpl Bev Baldwin
2Lt Joe Bales
Lt Todd Balfe
Capt Alan "Bam Bam" Bampton
Cpl Rick Banks
Capt Steve Bannister
Maj Michael Bannon
Cpl John Barnhardt
MCpl Fred Barrett
Cpl Jim "Batman" Bateman
Lt Oliver "Oman" Baus
Capt "Beards" Beardsley
Pte Jeff Beasley
Sgt Colin Beattie
Cpl Devon Beaudry
MCpl Wilfred Beckwith
Capt Rick Bedard
Lt Dave Beerman
Lt Alain Belanger
Cpl Jim Beresford
Lt Rick Berti
Maj Mike Bertrand

2Lt Marlene Berghout
Capt Sylvain Besner
OCdt Ed Bessada
2Lt Mike Biehl
Capt Marc Bigaouette
Capt Ron Bissonette
Capt Dean Black
Capt J.F. Blais
Capt Pierre Blais
Capt Denis Blanchet
Capt Philippe Bleau
Lt Paul Blouin
Lt Dave Bluhm
Capt Orlando Bokor
Capt Ulrich Bollinger
MCpl Ken Booth
Capt Dan Bouchard
Maj Pierre Bouchard
MCpl Serge Bouchard
Michael Bourque
Col John Boyle
Mary Jane Bradley
Capt Dan Brennan
Capt Bill "Bronco" Brown
Capt Jeff Brown
OCdt Joel Brown
MCpl Ted Brown
Col Bill Bucham
Maj Eric Burke
MCpl Jim Burke
Sid Burke
Capt Rob Burns
Lt Fred Burow
Maj Dave "DC" Burt
Cpl Jim Burton
Cpl John Burton
Maj Bob Butt
Capt Sean "Burner" Byrne

Capt Jay Campbell
Maj Peter Campbell
Sgt Ron Candow
OCdt Frank Cannon
Maj Dave Carmichael
Maj Simon Carr
Sgt Ed Carroll
Sgt Phil Cashman
Sgt Don Cassidy
MCpl Paul Caughy

Capt Jack Cavanas (Belgian Air Force)
Lt Glen Chamberlain
LCol Bill "Tatu" Charlton
Cpl Karen Chase
Capt Randy Chaulk
MCpl Maurice Chausse
Lt Gary Chesham
Cpl "Chev" Cheverie
Cpl Yves Chevier
Capt Brock Chisholm
MCpl Eric Choptian
2Lt Chris Coates
Cpl Alvin Cole
Cpl Roger Cole
LCol John Cody
MCpl Michel Collette
Sgt Phil Comeau
Cpl Ron Condly
Maj Chas Cormier
Cpl Marc Cossette
Lt Rob Coulthard
Capt T.R. "Throb" Cox
Capt Ken Craig
MCpl Richard Cuchesne
Capt Bob Curran
Capt Dan Cybulski
Capt Mike Czirjak

WO Dakim
Col Duane Daly
Capt Wayne Davidson
Cpl Mark Davies
Maj Dawson
Lt John Deboer
OCdt Bruce "Digger" Degeer
Capt Sluggo Demers
Maj Dan Dempsey
MCpl Paul Dennis
MCpl Doug Dennison
LCol Len Dent
Lt Claire Derepentigny
Capt Pierre "Dez" Desbiens
Cpl Mario Deshaies
Cpl Guy Desrosiers
Cdt Paul De Vesel (Belgian Air Force)
Cpl Mark Dick
Sgt Dyx Dickson

Cpl Blair Dirks
MCpl Gerry Dominie
Lt (N) Mark Donnelly
Cpl Don Dorval
Cpl Barry Doyle
LCol Bert Doyle
Lt Chris Drouin
Lt Richard Drouin
MCpl Richard Duchesne
MCpl Alain Dufour
Lt Jacques Dufour
Cpl Don Dumphy
Maj Tim Dunne
WO Martin Dupuis

Capt Allan Edgar
Lt Jeff Edey
Cpl Kerwin Elliot
Wes Embanks

Brent Fearon
WO Vic Fehr
Pte Robert Felder
Capt Ross Fetterly
Capt Paul Fleet
Pte Harvey Flowers
Cpl Dennis Fontaine
Sean Fordyce
Sgt Bob Forgues
MCpl Guy Fortin
Pam Forward
Capt Michel Fournier
Maj Jeff Foss
Cpl Pat Fox
Lt Ian Frei

Capt Norm Gagné
Lt Francois Gagnon
MS Steve Galbraith
MCpl Al Gallant
Cpl Darcy Gallipeau
Cpl Dave Garlick
WO Phil Garvin
Sgt Gilbert Gaudreault
MCpl Reg Gauthier
Cpl Rob Gauthier
Capt Kevin Gawne
Capt Bo Geddes
Lt Stephane Giardin
Capt Catherine Gibson
Capt Mike Gibson

Cpl "Seat Check" Gilchrist
Pte Tom Girardin
Cpl Dan Globensky
Capt Chris "Gloves" Glover
Maj Jim Glover
MCpl Ben Godin
Cpl Kevin Goodlad
Capt Mike Gorrell
Cpl Glenn Gray
Capt Rod Gray
Air Cdt Jason Grenier
OCdt Ray Grenkow
MCpl Ben Godin
S/L Steve Gorton (RAF)
Capt André Guay
LCol Ron Guidinger
Cpl Alain Gunville
MCpl Nora Gurzinski

Capt Dale Hackett
George Hall
Capt Duncan Handley
Capt Pete Handy
MCpl Geoff Harbinson
Maj Darryl Harden
Maj Rick Hardy
S/L Chris "Harps" Harper (RAF)
Cpl Donald Harper
Cpl Ivan Harvey
Capt R.M. "Eddie" Haskins
LCol Laurie "Hawnski" Hawn
Capt John Haazen
MCpl Brent Hart
Cpl Pat Heald
Cpl Brian Helpard
Capt Walter Heneghan
LCol Csaba Hezsely
Cpl Robert High
WO Bill Hill
Col D.F. Holman
OCdt Derrick Hotte
Capt Danny Houde
Maj Peter Howe
F/Sgt Michelle Hubert (Air Cdts)
WO George Hughes
Lt Grant Hughes

LCol D.F. "Yogi" Hyghebaert
Capt Janet Hynes

Lt Gordon Ireland

Capt Nigel Jackson
MCpl Alex Jardine
LCol Ed Jay
Cpl Leo Jenkins
CWO Paul Jenkins
Capt Rob Jenkins
Capt Rob Jewett
Sgt Fred "AJ" Jodoin
WO Vic Johnson
Capt Trevor Jones
Col D.M. Jurkowski

Capt Chris Kay
Maj Dave "DW" Kendall
Sgt Sean Kennedy
Capt "Mich" Kerckhofs (Belgian AF)
Lt Paul Kidner
Lt Randy King
Maj Kirk Kirkpatrick
Col. W.R. Bill Kirkwood
Capt Bjorn Kjaer
Capt Tom Klassen
Capt Kevin Kokotailo
Lt Tom Kolesnik
Michael Krauss
CWO Bill Krier
Lt Wade Kropelin
Capt Jimmy "Bugs" Kyle

Lt Serge Lacasse
Maj Tony Laface
MCpl Barry Lake
LCol Bob "Du Lac" Lake
Capt Christian Lalande
Col Bernie Laliberte
Pte Chris Lalonde
Pvt Corey Lamothe
Capt Normand Landry
WO Don Lane
Sgt Bob Lang
Capt "Bunny" Larocque
Pte Jim Larocque
Capt "Bingo" Larue
Maj Richard Larouche
Lt Julie Lauzon
Capt John Latulippe
Lt Richard Lavallee
Capt Gary Le Bouthillier
Maj Terry Leversedge
WO Ron Lavoi
Capt Tery Lebel
Capt Don Leblanc
Sgt Joe Leblanc
Capt Roger Leblanc
WO Smokie Leblanc
Rick Lee
MCpl Cliff Lefrense
Maj J.F. Legare

OCdt Steve Le Gassick
Capt Dan Legault
Capt Mike Lenehan
Air Cdt Mathew Lewis
Capt Perry Lewis
Col Hubert Leduc
LCol Clark "Boss" Little
Cpl Oswald Lindsay
Cpl Doug Lloyd
Capt Rick "Mongo" Lloyd
Capt Michael Lopianowski
Lt Greg Lot
Capt John Low
Sgt Derek Luczak
Cpl Jeffrey Lukasik
Capt Hans "King" Lund (Norwegian AF)
MCpl Denis Lyons

Maj Mike MacDonald
Capt Neil MacDonald
Maj Hugh Mackay
Sgt Mario Marcotte
MWO Bob Martel
MCpl Gilles Martel
Capt Brock Martin
Capt Frank Martineau
MCpl Bo Massz
Cpl Chris Matte
Capt Mike Mawson
Capt Mike Mayhew
Lt Christine McCarthy
Lt Don McClellan
Capt Karen McCrimmon
Sgt John McCullough
LCol Earl McCurdy
Capt Larry McCurdy
MCpl Dave McDonald
2Lt Will McEwan
MCpl Bob McGrath
Lt Tedd McHenry
Lt Al McMillan
Cpl Glenn McNaughton
PO2 Dermot Meade
Capt Francis Mercier
Capt Bill Michael
Maj Randy Meiklejohn
Maj Don Middleton
Sgt Bill Moody
MCpl Kevin Morowski
MCpl John Moss
WO Joe Monkhouse
Sgt Dave Moriarty
Lt Sylvie Morin
Cpl Jeff Morris
Maj Bill Motriuk
Lt Mulineaux
MCpl Wendy Muehlgassner
Pte Rob Muraca
Maj Brian Myrah
Cpl Bernard Myron

Cpl Gordon Neave
Capt Louise Neil
Col D.E. Nicoll
Capt Daniel Noebert
LCol Leo Nolan

BGen Dave O'Blenis
Capt Geoff Oborne
LCol O'Brien
Cpl Shelley Oel
Capt John Oja
Maj Lawrence O'Neill
MCpl Bob O'Reilly
Maj Paul O'Reilly
Cpl Ron O'Reilly
Capt Rob Orme
Cpl Frank Ouellet

Sgt Michel Papineau
LCol Joe Paquette
CWO Guy Parent
Cpl Ken Parent
Capt Rudy Parent
Pte Gaetan Parr
Lt Steve Parry
Maj Al Paul
Sgt Joanne "Camera Snags" Paul
Maj John Pearson
LCol Ken Pennie
Pte Darrel Peterson
Capt Van "Poncho" Peterson
WO Rene Phaneuf
Sgt Lou Phillips
Capt Kevin Pickett
Capt Dan Poirier
Capt Jim Pollitt
Capt Tom Potter
MCpl Ken Power
Capt Miles Pratt
Capt "Sunny" Pshebylo
F/O Bill Purcello (ret)

Lt Line Quiron

Capt Les Racicot
Capt Terry Rahn
LS Rob Rawn
OCdt Jim Rees
Lt Paul "Rigs" Regli
Maj Ike Reid
MCpl Claude Richard
Maj Dave Richards
MCpl Bruce Richmond
OCdt Stephan Robidoux
Capt Kevin Roberts
Lt Stephen Roberts
Maj Pierre Rochefort
Lt Alain Rochette
Capt Mike Rode
Lt Blair Roe
LCol Dick Rogers
Capt Jeff "Buck" Rogers
LCol Stan Rolsky
Cpl Mark Rootes

WO Bob Ross
WO Lloyd Ross
Lt Joan Rowell
Maj Claude Roy
Capt Pierre Ruel
Sgt Reg Russell
Maj Veejay Ryan

Maj Brian "BJ" Salmon
OCdt Steven Sarty
MCpl Dave Saverin
Capt Andre Sauve
Maj Rick Savin
Cpl Dave Scharf
Capt Peter Scheidler
Cpl Don Schoenenberger
John Schultz
Lt Bob Schwartz
MCpl Craig Seager
WO Tom Secretan
Capt Bob Selleck
Cpl Steve Seymour
Lt Shaun Shanahan
Capt Mike Sharon
Lt Andre Shank
WO Ron Shaw
Cpl Don Shears
Cpl Chris Sheppard
Capt Greg "Shep" Shepherd
Cpl Drew Sherwood
Capt Darryl Shyiak
Cpl Gary Sideen
Capt Marc Simard
MCpl Mike Simpson
Capt Wayne Sinker
Maj Jim Skinner
Cpl Patsy Slapsys
LCol Smith
Capt Gord Smith
Capt Bill Snedden
Lt Brent Sparks
Capt Jeff Sparkes
Sgt Bill Spellman
Maj Terry Spraggs
Sgt Gary Spurrell
Capt Bob Stephan
Pte Anne Stevenson
Capt Kevin "Stewie" Stewart
WO John Stirton
Capt Brian "Stoker" Stooke
Capt Martha Stouffer
Cpl Wayne Stoyles
Cpl John Stuart
Maj "Duff" Sullivan
Capt Kirk Sunter
Capt Wally Sweetman

Capt Camil Taillefer
Capt Dominic Taillon
Capt Tom "Jaws" Taylor
Cpl Steve Tedema

Capt Paul Tesseyman
Capt Joe Theberge
Maj Ed Theoret
Col Claude "Stretch" Thibault
Capt Brian Thomas
Cpl John Thompson
Capt Neil Thomsen
Capt Dennis Thornton
LCol Eric Thurston
Cpl Pat Tighe
Maj Bill Todd
Rafe Tomsett
Capt Rick "Ricardo" Traven
Maj Yves Tremblay
Pte Cheryl Truman
LCol Bill Turnbull

Maj Ed Ukrainetz
Sgt Jerry Unrau

Cpl Avril Van Aert
Capt Paul Vander Basch
Capt John Van Oosten
Capt Kent Vanvliet

Maj Bob Wade
Sgt Husam Wafaei
Capt Ray Wagstaff
Capt Craig "Wally" Waldick
MCpl Joe Walsh
LCol Fred Walt
Pte Rowan Walters
Cpl Kimberly Ward
Cpl Warren Webber
MCpl Wayne Webster
Maj Bill Werny
Pte Steve Wetmore
Capt Tony White
LCol Trevor White
Maj Bart Wickham
Capt Clive Wilkins
Capt Stephen Will
OCdt Steven Williams
WO Willie Williams
Capt Rick Wilson
Capt Sue Witchel
2Lt Stephan Wood
Capt Ross Wuerth

Cpl Michael Yates
Lt Linda Yurkiew

Capt Larry Zadan
Robert E. Lennox

SNOWBIRDS

TRAINING

BOOST CHECK, CHANGE CHECK-CHECK, RICH-HOT-BOTH,

try start, no start, Mayday-Mayday-Mayday, DAL transmit on, 3 off, 2 off, brakes off,
harness tight, In We Go . . . . . –Musketeer forced landing check

raining Group is, as the name
implies, the organization within the
Canadian Air Force responsible for
training. Apart from aircrew training, the
Group also prepares all the technical
specialists and air-traffic controllers in
addition to managing a myriad of other
air-related instructional programs.

MUSKETEER

CT-134

Our training here is roughly the equivalent of the first half of a private pilot's license in the civilian world, but I've seen guys with a commercial pilot's license dropped from this course. They call it "cease training" or CT and, to a student pilot, there is no more dreaded phrase in the English language. The standards and rates of progression are unbelievably high, and the reasoning makes sense. Our instructors always say that, given enough time, they could teach a monkey to fly. But they want only the absolute best people leaving here to go to jets at Moose Jaw. They want pilots who can learn fast, make good decisions quickly and handle pressure. They would rather CT ten good candidates than let an average one slip through, so they go about their task ruthlessly.

They tell us that during World War II, Canada, through the Commonwealth Air Training Plan, trained 155,000 air crew for Allied air forces. Standards were high then, and I guess they don't see any reason for things to change. Their attitude seems to be that if you are going to teach people to fly, they might as well be good at it.

One of my earlier trips is a perfect example. On leave, before coming to Portage, I did ten hours of instruction at my local flying club and I figured I was ahead of the game. My first few trips went great, but on this particular flight I was told to climb out at 90 kts. I felt I was close enough holding 88 kts with everything else pegged. The instructor hooked me with a cold stare and advised that it was bad enough I was not at the requested airspeed but, even worse, was the fact that I knew I was 2 kts under and had done nothing to correct it. As I was absorbing that slap he pulled the power on me and things really started piling up. My landing was so bad the ground crew asked my instructor if he wanted to call the MP's and have me charged with attempted murder. When we have one of those flights where the brain overloads and wants to lock up we call it "havin' a helmet fire."

B ut I know I'll make it to Moose Jaw. I've learned from my mistakes and I can do it. And I've had my dunk in the tub right out there on the flight line. That comes right after you solo and it's the best bath you will ever have. So now it's five more tests and I'm on my way to where I've always wanted to be – fast with a mask and upside down.

A Student Pilot – Musketeers

JET RANGER
CH-139

I asked to come here to Portage, to instruct on the Jet Rangers. It's turned out to be a great tour. I spent four years flying Twin Hueys in a Tac Hel squadron and the flying was superb, but in my last year alone I accumulated 250 days away from home. The system was eating me up. I had absolutely no social life and the idea of being able to actually plan a weekend off was a real attraction to this tour of duty. Now I'm a member of the Toastmasters, a minor hockey referee and I even have the chance to make a date once in a while.

But the real excitement here is seeing a student – fresh from the pressure cooker Basic Jet Course – solo a rotary wing aircraft after just 11 hours on the helicopter. We put about 40 to 45 people through a year and the atmosphere is much more relaxed than what the student has experienced in his Musketeer and Tutor phases. That's not to say that he'll have a lot of spare time while he's here. In just three short months he'll become fully qualified on a turbine helicopter. That means absorbing a fair amount of knowledge, not to mention a whole new set of hand-eye skills. In the beginning some of these people are not too thrilled with having been selected to go helicopter. But by the time we pin a new set of wings on their chests they're all for the rotary world and full of derisive comments for any pilot who can't "hover ."

And then there's the historical aspect. The Air Force has been training pilots at this base for over 50 years. I really like the feeling of being a part of that tradition. If these runways could only talk.

For every wings class we get a "posting block" from Ottawa that lists pilot vacancies by aircraft type. That's: "Kiowa, Single" or "Twin Huey, Chinook, Labrador" or "Sea King." Usually we let the graduates sort out amongst themselves which aircraft they would like to be assigned to. Then the instructors, in a posting meeting, match the students' performance and aptitudes with their requests before the final slots are filled. Over 50 per cent get their first choice.

Another advantage our students have stems from the requirement that all our instructors must have an operational tour under their belt before coming here. That means that whatever aircraft type a student is interested in he will probably have access to someone who has flown it before. That way he can get first-hand information about what it's really like from someone who knows.

I he Bell 206B Jet Rangers we use
here at the school couldn't be more
suited to the job. They are turbine
engined, as are all the helicopters in use
throughout the Air Force, so the pilots
are already familiar with this technology
when they arrive at their operational
squadrons. The engines and transmis-
sions are tough and reliable, the aircraft
is very forgiving and it's a dream to fly.
What more could you ask for?

A Helicopter Instructor – Jet Rangers

TUTOR
CT-114

Aircrew Selection in Downsview, the officers course in Chilliwack, language school in St. Jean, mark time waiting for courses in several places, then Musketeers in Portage and, finally, Moose Jaw and jets! And the pressure point was always the same – make the grade or you're out. Even flying the Musketeers was considered the last part of the "selection" process. The pressure here is, in many ways, even more intense but there is one key distinction. Now they are finally trying to make pilots out of us rather than trying to get rid of us. It makes all the difference and I love it. Now I am not the only human being on the planet that wants me to leave here wearing wings.

A Basic Jet Course Student-Tutors

AIR CADETS

F/SGT **JACQUES DUFORT**, RCAC

LT **JACQUES DUFORT**, HERCULES PILOT

As a CIL officer (Cadet Instructor List) my duties centre on flying the tow plane in the Cadet Gliding Program. One of the plums an air cadet can strive for is a flying scholarship which will enable him or her to obtain a Department of Transport Glider Pilot license.

CAPT **SUE WITCHEL,** INSTRUCTOR, JETS

F/SGT **SUE WITCHEL,** RCAC

The young people who go through this program are an absolute delight to work with and I look forward to my flying weekends now as much as I used to relish strapping into the cockpit of my Voodoo a few years back.

CAPT **STEVE WILL,** SNOWBIRD PILOT

WO **STEVE WILL,** RCAC

I he Air Cadet Program provides
young people with an opportunity to improve themselves
in a number of ways. One of these is
through the summer camps and it is
here that a handful of cadets enrolled in
the glider program join hundreds of
others actively engaged in a number of
courses. The
atmosphere and
style is naturally
military and while
cadets often go on
to careers in the
Canadian Armed
Forces we are not
a recruiting organi-
zation. Our goal is
simply to help build
better citizens.

WO1 **JEFF EDEY,** RCAC

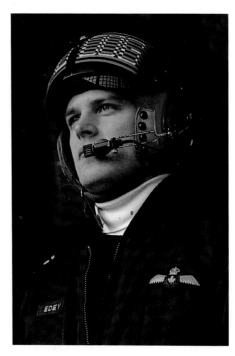

LT **JEFF EDEY,** KIOWA PILOT

Nothing brings this point home more than standing on the sidelines of a summer camp graduation parade. I had this privilege on a perfect August evening in Trenton and I heartily recommend it to anyone who harbours doubts about the quality of our younger generation. Imagine over 900 fine young boys and girls assembled in one place, standing proudly at attention, eyes bright in the glow of their own personal accomplishments and adventures. This is what it's all about.

A Cadet Instructor

10 TAG

TEN TACTICAL AIR GROUP

The 10 Tactical Air Group (10 TAG) is the arm of the Canadian Air Force providing helicopter support to the Canadian Armed Forces Mobile Command. These combat-trained squadrons are equipped with Kiowas, Twin Hueys and Chinooks and fulfil a variety of roles as elements of the Canadian Tactical Helicopters (Tac Hel) capability.

TWIN HUEY

CH-135

Our Twin Hueys operate in UTH or utility tactical transport helicopter flights. They are tasked with moving troops and equipment to forward areas and with casualty evacuation. We can load up to 11 fully armed troopers into the back or sling up to 2900 pounds. This can amount to a 105mm pack howitzer or a jeep.

The big advantage to flying Hueys in the Canadian Air Force is that we get to do everything rather than specializing in a particular aspect of helicopter flying. As a result we are kept busy mastering and maintaining our skills in airmobile assaults, hoisting and slinging, low-level flying and navigation, dropping paratroopers, fire fighting, rappelling and utility flying.

Pilots going "rotary" do their Wings course on Tutors and Jet Rangers. Then, like all pilots, we go to an OTU (operational training unit) squadron for instruction on a particular aircraft type. For Twin Hueys this is Gagetown. They told us we would start our navigation work at 500 feet, then we'd move down to 200 feet, and very shortly thereafter, down to where the Huey really belongs – 15 feet.

We fly with two pilots and a flight engineer (FE). The FE is really a technical advisor. He knows everything about the airframe and engine and tells us whether we can fly or not. A lot of them have at least 10 years experience on the hangar floor and we rely on them completely. Often I hear a little noise or feel a funny little vibration and first thing I do is ask the FE for his opinion. If he tells me he's happy and not to worry about it, we go flying. No problem.

Aside from lots of good flying, us Huey pilots see a larger variety of duty stations. Most of us get six-month tours with the Multinational Force and Observers (MFO) in the Sinai. With the MFO we're operational and are exposed to another world. A world very different from what we're used to in Canada.

The MFO is in place to supervise the peace agreement between Israel and Egypt. It's our job to provide transport support to the civilian observers who oversee the Israeli and Egyptian positions to ensure compliance with the treaty. Our only enemies there are the sand and the heat. But once again, our maintenance people work their usual miracles. They give us serviceable aircraft that allow us to fulfil our commitment, despite the difficult environment.

A Twin Huey Pilot

TECH

AIRFRAME/AERO ENGINE TECHNICIAN

The great thing about working Tactical Helicopter (Tac Hel) is that we get to do both airframe and aero engine work, so we get to know the whole machine. In the military units of other countries a technician will often specialize in just the airframe or the engine.

Another thing about Tac Hel is the added challenge of field mainten- ance. When the squadron deploys to the field we're right out there with them in the bush, keeping the airplanes flying. We live in tents and have to be prepared to work in mud or snow, out of canvas hangars or right out in the elements. We have a saying: Never has so much been done by so few with so little. But we like the satisfaction that comes with keeping our helicopters serviceable no matter what the condi- tions. And our units are small, which makes for great spirit.

Our signature in the aircraft log means one of two things. Either the airplane is not going to fly, or the airplane is not going to crash.

An Airframe/Aero Engine Technician – Tac Hel

CHINOOK
CH-147

The Chinook is the Air Force's heavy
lifter providing logistical transport
support to land forces. Apart from
moving personnel and material
"forward," it has the heavy lift capability

KIOWA
CH-136

We call it "nap of the earth" or NOE and this is what makes Kiowa flying so much fun. A helicopter's survival in combat is directly related to how low it flies. Low and fast makes it tough to shoot and we spend three months and about 100 hours in the air to master the techniques. Other aircraft types have minimums expressed numerically in feet, but us LOH (pronounced *loach*) drivers fly as low as vegetation permits. We call it "skids clear of vegetation." It's exhilarating. It's demanding. It's the joy of flying in its purest form!

The Kiowa is tactically deployed as an LOH or light observation helicopter. It performs a number of critical duties for a battlefield commander including artillery and fighter fire direction or spotting. When we work for the artillery we are an air observation post, while the Air Force calls us forward air controllers. When we locate and direct fire on enemy positions we have to operate on or behind the front lines and the enemy will make every effort to create a "bad day" for us.

The Kiowa's main armament is a 7.62 machine gun slung down from the belly. It's strictly defensive and of limited effect since its 450 pounds place severe strain on a relatively under-powered machine. We can also carry six 2.75 inch Mk. 1V rockets, but these are solely for marking targets. In a high-threat environment, where the enemy is likely to have tanks, surface-to-air missiles, heavily armed attack helos (like the Soviet Hind), and fast air and con-ventional small arms fire, we'll fall back on our NOE skills and our radar warning receiver (RWR) to direct us. The RWR will emit a tone and give us a visual indication when we have been "acquired" by an enemy weapon. Then it's crank and bank time. One advantage is that we're small and covered with a special radar reflective paint so we don't "paint" all that well on enemy radar. But our best defence is our agility and ability to hide behind natural objects. We can get lost in ground clutter.

We also have a limited casualty evacua-tion and heliborne resupply function as well as photo reconnaissance capabilities. Our command and liaison duties mean getting commanders to battlefield meetings on time. Just call us high speed, cross country, all-terrain jeeps!

The Kiowa is a single-pilot airplane, but we fly with a LOH observer in the left seat. He stays with us for two years and brings with him valuable ground experience acquired in combat arms with the army. An enlisted man, he performs many of the same duties as pilots in other aircraft types. He's trained to handle the radios, to call in artillery and fast air strikes and to navigate for the pilot.

Navigation is particularly demanding in Tac Hel flying. We're operating at very low altitudes so there aren't a lot of references within his (the observer's) line of vision. I compare it to infantry-type map reading, but at 90 kts the pace is a little more intense. When we're booking along on or below the treetops the observer will constantly be telling me what to expect over the next ridge or around the bend of the stream we're following. At the same time, he has to be looking for the enemy units and be mentally prepared to fix their position for our forces, he has to keep an ear tuned to the radar warning set, and he has to keep an eye out for the best places for us to hide when the need arises. I count on him to give me all the information. He counts on me to keep us flying. This is team flying at its best and just another one of the many attractions of Kiowa flying.

A Kiowa Pilot

AETE
AEROSPACE ENGINEERING TEST ESTABLISHMENT

Right now we have more than 60 separate projects underway within the organization, so it's tough to pick out a favourite. But if I had to, I think it would be the software updates I'm currently involved with on the F-18.

Most of our work comes from air crew suggestions. In this case a pilot thought it would be great if the computers on the Hornet could tell him his time on target and auto-sequence his remaining way points. So that's what we are working towards achieving. Our biggest player, as we call it, is what the people in the cockpits feel would make their lives easier and safer.

Our job is testing airplanes and their components. Part of that is making sure that equipment purchased or modified for the Air Force will do what the manufacturer says it will, for the length of time required. The other side is working up improvements to existing material in the inventory. Many of our aircraft are approaching the end of their service lives and we come up with modification programs to extend the hours these machines can continue to fly until replacements are acquired.

We also test aircraft under consideration for purchase by the Department of National Defence to insure they will work in our environment. A perfect example of the necessity of looking at a particular aircraft in an environmental context can be found in early problems we had with the tail assembly on the CF-18.

McDonnell Douglas designed the jet for the US Navy and Marines and the mission profiles included a lot of transit time mixed into the high G, high-stress ACM activity. When we fly the airplanes we have very little transit time in comparison, getting right into high G training manoeuvres. This different way of

operating the machine showed up in the tail assemblies. Six cleats in the vertical stabilizers together with a special "fence" on the leading edge extension of the wing solved the problem.

Our fleet of fixed and rotary-winged aircraft numbers over 20 at the moment and includes over 15 of the 21 aircraft types currently in the Air Force inventory. It makes for an interesting hangar and terrific variety for the people who work here. And there are about 350 of us divided up amongst test pilots, engineers and specialists, in every imaginable field of aviation.

A Test Pilot – Aerospace Engineering
Test Establishment

TRANSPORT

Air Transport Group's task is to provide airlift capacity to the Canadian government in support of the defence of Canada or in response to emergency relief efforts anywhere in the world. ATG is also called upon to deploy for search and rescue missions over land and water.

HERCULES
CC-130

The fighter jocks call us trash haulers but that trash is usually essential material and often it can mean the difference between life and death.

There's a sort of mystique to flying a Hercules. It's been around for 30 years and I understand Lockheed plans to keep building them well into the 1990's. Some of our airplanes are on their second or even third set of wings with over 20,000 hours on the airframes, but they just keep right on keepin' on.

After you fly them up north in our Arctic environment for a while, going in and out of gravel strips like Alert with not so much as a skipped beat, it's real easy to develop a special confidence in the airplane. The gravel doesn't bother our props like it would a jet engine and no other propeller airplane can carry the load of our Hercs.

Gross takeoff weight is a hefty 155,000 pounds and she weighs 75,000 empty which means she can carry her own weight in fuel and cargo. Her engines burn 5,000 pounds of fuel per hour at cruise and we can pump 62,000 pounds into her, so there's not too many places we can't get to.

The search and rescue scenario that best illustrates the beauty of the Herc centres on what would happen if a commercial airliner was forced down in the Canadian Arctic. We have shells of food, clothing, medicine and shelters ready to be loaded onto Hercs and air-dropped onto the crash site along with our search and rescue technicians. Then, if need be, we could fly in a bulldozer, drop it, and circle overhead while they carved out a runway for us to land on.

And where else can a 24-year-old pilot get left-seat or command time in a large aircraft and experience such a variety of hands on flying situations? To start with, every one of us gets a "Global Trainer" at some point in our tour. This means we take off heading east or west and keep right on going until we get back to the base. We fly around the world in about two weeks, re-supplying Canadian embassies and military installations.

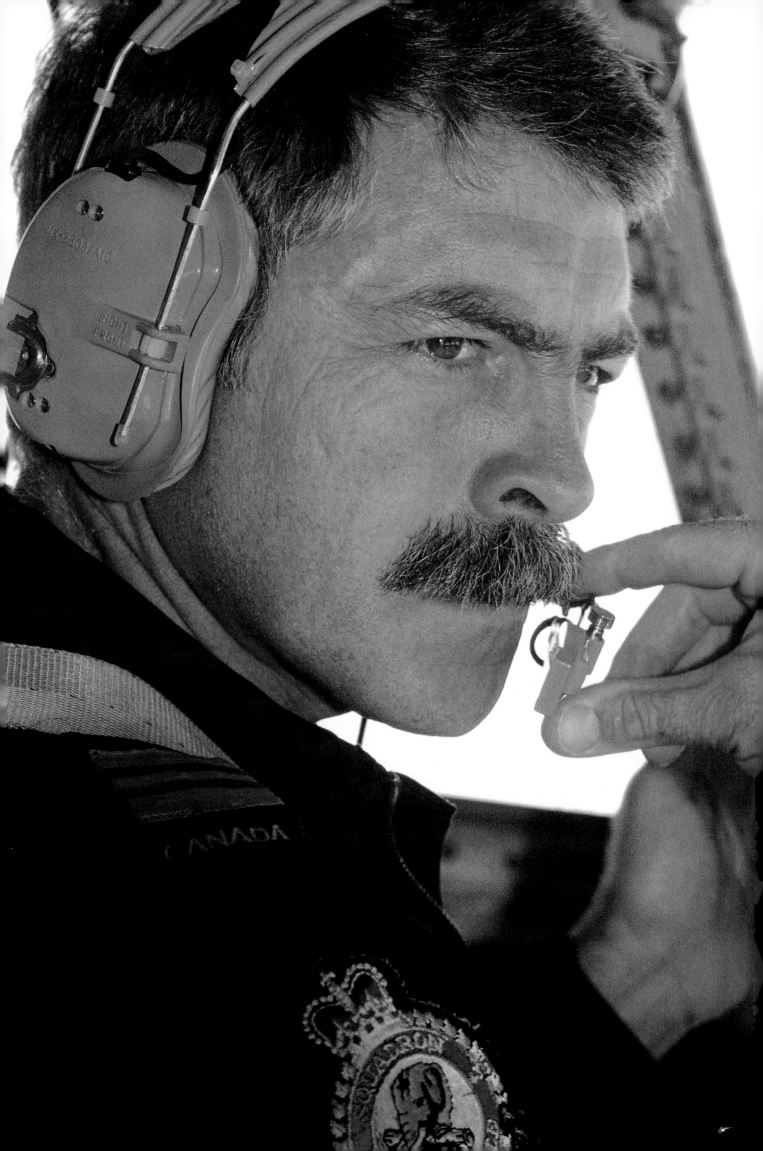

On top of this we have primary responsibility when Canada provides disaster relief to trouble spots anywhere in the world. Recently our aircraft have flown relief supplies to Ethiopia, Iran, Jamaica, Armenia and South America. A lot of missions require us to bore holes in the sky for upwards of 10 or 11 hours and our crew days can exceed 20 hours. But it's all worthwhile when you get to see the look on people's faces after you've flown in a couple of tons of clothing and food when they haven't had any for a few days.

And then there's the tactical side. Dropping paratroopers or maybe a low-level contour approach followed by a LAPES (low altitude parachute extraction system) drop out the back at ten feet. Then it's stay on the deck and back to the airport with an overhead break to land fast.

Sometimes I think it might be nice to be going through Mach-8 in one of our Challengers eatin' shrimp salad and watching a movie, but I could never leave the Hercs. Fat, dumb and friendly is what they call us. It works for me.

A Hercules Pilot

LABRADOR
CH-113

SEARCH & RESCUE

Ihe chance to save a life, that's why we're here. To even apply for Search and Rescue (SAR) you have to have another trade, be at least a corporal, and just plain want it more than anything else in the world.

For my course I was one of 10 selected from a field of 841 applicants. And that was after applying three years straight. But I never wanted to do anything else in the military. SAR is a career position in the Air Force, so I'll be doing this until the day I pull the pin. And if I save just one life in that time it will have been more than worth it. It'll make up for all the bad ones where there are no survivors.

Our primary job as SAR Techs is to assist in locating downed aircraft and then go into the crash site as soon as possible and save lives. If our helicopter can't land we'll go down by hoist, and if that's not an option we'll jump in. We also respond to ships in distress, lost hikers or any human being that needs our help.

In SAR we're cross-trained in a number of areas such as parachuting, diving, medical training and load mastering. And we are prepared to operate in any type of environment from Arctic ice flows to the Rockies.

As a unit we rely on each other to a greater extent than they do in other military units. The usual barrier between officers and enlisted men is blurred here. A "debrief" means all ranks let down a bit around the beer fridge. We don't have any professional counselling, so after a bad one, when you're a little shook up, you toss it back and forth with the troops, drink a beer or two and it gets sorted out. You get past it and keep your edge.

But the job has its lighter side. In Canada most aircraft have an emergency locater transmitter which is designed to transmit a radio homing signal if its host aircraft crashes. Like any piece of equipment it needs maintenance from time to time. Once a pilot casually tossed his into the trunk of his car and headed off to have it serviced. But unknown to this guy, the toss was just hard enough to set the thing off and the resulting distress signal was immediately monitored by our Rescue Co-ordination Centre. Thirteen minutes later we were airborne in a C-130 looking for the source. It wasn't long before we had a black Mustang on the 401 identified as the culprit. I wish I could have seen the look on the driver's face when we buzzed him with the Herc. He figured it out after the second pass and pulled over to shut it off.

When we launch for an ELT signal it's always fun when our pilot figures out that it's moving. We know we will end up chasing a train, postal truck or car, that there is no crash site to hunt for because crash sites rarely move.

But we utilize opportunities like this to do some training. Every time we launch we get just a little bit faster than the time before and it all contributes to keeping our edge. Keeping that edge means training and we do it every day. We get a lot of time in our main aircraft– Buffalo, Labrador, Hercules and Twin Otter. That's just fine with me because I love flying, love getting out and doing it, love my job.

A SAR Tech

BUFFALO
CC-115

458

CAUTION

DO NOT PLUG OR DEFORM HOLES
AREA WITHIN RED BAND MUST
BE KEPT CLEAN AND SMOOTH

When General Manson, former Chief of Defence Staff, characterized Search and Rescue flying as being some of the most challenging in the Air Force today, he wasn't just whistling the Air Force march past. Military flying in peacetime centres entirely on training for the day the balloon goes up. SAR is our battlefield and we go to war almost every day.

Our primary duty is to locate lost souls and if there's one thing I've noticed over the years it's that pilots almost never get into trouble on nice sunny afternoons. Miserable weather is invariably involved, not to mention adverse circumstances such as the loss of the Ocean Ranger, with all hands, off Newfoundland in February of 1983. But the amount of time we spend flying in crud, those call-ups in the middle of the night and the often tragic aspects of our work are all forgotten when we make the difference between someone's living and dying. That is job satisfaction that you just can't measure.

The Buffalo is an excellent SAR platform whether you're yanking and banking down in the weeds or putting it into a short strip. Every airplane has something it does best, it's signature manoeuvre, and for the Buff that is unquestionably it's STOL (short take-off and landing) ability. And it's impressive whether you're in the cockpit or on the ground. I love doing airshows with this airplane because I know I'll wax the zoomies in their high-priced jets every time. The STOL landing is our show stealer. We start at about 1500 feet by hanging 41,000 pounds of hardware right on the edge, in a pro-

nounced nose-down attitude, point it at the end of the runway and then grind her to a full-stop in a little under 500 feet. The crowd roars and the Stanley Cup is ours again.

A Buffalo Pilot

TWIN OTTER
CC-138

The de Havilland Twin Otter is a light short take-off and landing (STOL) utility transport aircraft. It is used primarily in Search and Rescue but also provides a transport role as well as support to the Air Force's northern operations.

DASH 8
CC-142

The Dash 8 is a turbo-prop transport designed and manufactured by de Havilland Aircraft of Canada. Two of these are currently providing transport service in Germany and an additional four have been delivered to the Navigation Training School at CFB Winnipeg.

CHALLENGER
CC-144

The Canadair Challenger is a twin-jet executive transport utilized in the Air Force as a medium-to-long-range transport aircraft. It is also used as an electronic warfare (EW) training platform.

Fan Jet Falcon CC-117 currently being phased out by Challenger.

BOEING 707

CC-137

The Air Force's fleet of five Boeings has provided transport and air refueling support for 20 years. With current budgetary restraints preventing acquisition of a more modern replacement, they should be around for several more years.

COSMOPOLITAN
CC-109

T
he Cosmopolitan twin-engine turbo-prop transport was acquired in 1960 to replace the Dakota in Air Transport Command.

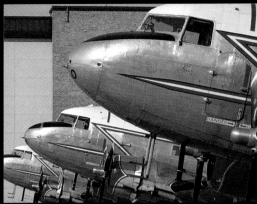

DAK
CC-129

A veteran of WW II, the Dak needs no introduction. On March 31, 1989 she was officially retired. The accompanying photographs were all taken at CFB Winnipeg during ceremonies commemorating the end of an era.

ATC
AIR TRAFFIC CONTROL

I love the daily challenge of air traffic control. When we are on duty we are operational. What I mean is we are not training for something that may happen in the future or playing video games. We deal with real airplanes in real time. These real airplanes come at us a lot faster than most civilian aircraft and most are streaking towards that little green dot in the centre of my screen. It's quite different from working in a civilian ATC environment where you deal with singles that are usually streamed into an arrival procedure following a very strict time schedule.

During our training we get experience in the control tower as well as in the radar room. Our larger bases have the new TRACS system in the radar room and mastering this latest technology is a real challenge. But we still have to be able to function in the event this equipment goes down or is disabled due to enemy action. We then revert to "procedural" controlling which means working without a scope or blind. We have to memorize about 60 different rules and apply them to maintain safe separation between targets that keep on moving in three dimensions. This is the part I found the toughest. But the double challenge of being both an air traffic controller and an officer makes for a lot of job satisfaction and that is what I was looking for.

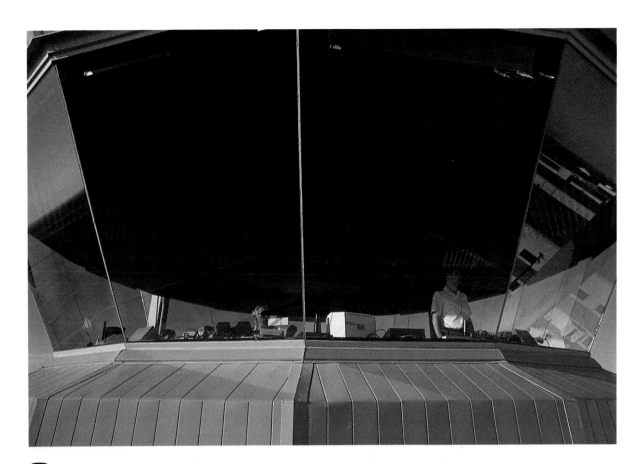

One of my proudest possessions is a certificate of commendation from Air Command given to me for saving the life of an CF-5 pilot. I was on duty when this guy took off with max fuel and ordnance but, just after rotating, he lost an engine to a compressor stall. He hit the burner on his remaining engine but it wasn't enough and I could see he was losing altitude and worse – I sensed his concentration was totally focused on recovering the airplane with no thought for ejecting. I told him to "Get out now!" And just as I said it the jet disappeared behind a tree line and then there was the inevitable fireball. Our base rescue Huey was air taxiing below the tower as all this was unfolding and he came on with a simple "I'm on the way." Unbelievably, a few moments later he came back with the news that he had spotted the pilot on the ground, alive.

Standard procedure after a crash is to replace the duty controller so they can run a series of blood tests to confirm that you were not under the influence of alcohol or drugs. After my tests at the hospital I ran into the pilot with his wife. He told me that the only thing he remembered of the entire accident was hearing that voice in his headset telling him to eject and then pulling the handle.

An Air Traffic Controller

MAG
MARITIME AIR GROUP

The primary responsibility of Maritime Air Group (MAG) is to provide Anti Submarine Warfare (ASW) protection to the Canadian Navy. MAG also flies sovereignty patrols over the Canadian Arctic in addition to supporting the Department of Fisheries and Oceans in its efforts to defend Canada's offshore fishing zones.

TRACKER
CP-121

We all have a lot of reasons to love the old Tracker, but the thing I always like to point out is that she'll fly underwater and through trees. We have film of a Tracker being launched off the *"Bonnie"* as the bow was headed down rather than on the upswing like the book says. The reasons for this are obvious. You either get cated up into some sky or down into some ocean. On this particular occasion the airplane actually flies straight through the big wave, coughs a couple of times coming out the other side, and continues to fly.

On a more personal level, I came into Saint John's a little low one night and felt a bump or two on short final. After I shut her down we discovered a little lumber stuck in the leading edge of the wing. The biggest piece was a solid 8 inches in diameter. In the morning we went up on the hill and found the swath she had cut through the forest.

Our Trackers, a de Havilland-built version of the Grumman S2, were made to be ridden hard and left wet. That's just what they've been doing for over 30 years in the Canadian Air Force. Selected originally for ASW work off the *Bonnie,* they were built a foot and a half shorter than the regular S2 so they'd fit in our carrier's hangar bays. The result of this shortening is a bigger moment which makes for a lively cockpit during single engine situations. At a critical airspeed of 85 kts the airplane requires 160 pounds of rudder pressure to keep her straight. But we have what we call a "single engine rudder assist" modification, which cuts this back to a relatively modest 50 pounds.

We fly the aircraft with two pilots and an AESOp (airborne electronic sensor operator) in the back. He operates our 360 Litton radar which is lowered down from the belly of the aircraft and allows us to search up to 50 miles at 1000 feet.

oday the Trackers are used mostly for surface surveillance in support of the Department of Fisheries and Oceans (DFO). We have a 200-mile offshore Economic Management Zone in which Canada controls the fishing. There's no problem finding this invisible line. You just fly due east until you spot a perfectly straight line of fishing boats and you'll know, without looking at a map, that you're there. These waters include the rich Grand Banks and a lot of foreign fishermen would love a free shot at working this area. If it weren't for our patrols they'd be there in force.

We record the position and the name of every vessel and cross check against our fishing license registry to verify that he's fishing legally. If he's not, we transmit this information to the Department of Fisheries people who can then direct surface vessels to the intruder. Often the captain can get out of our waters before DFO can intercept on the surface, but we will have photographed him and made a detailed – and legally verifiable – record of his position. Should that ship ever turn up at a Canadian port it could be confiscated and its captain and crew charged under Canadian law. It has happened often enough that we know our system works and, more important, these fishermen know it works. So our presence deters them from taking fish in Canadian waters.

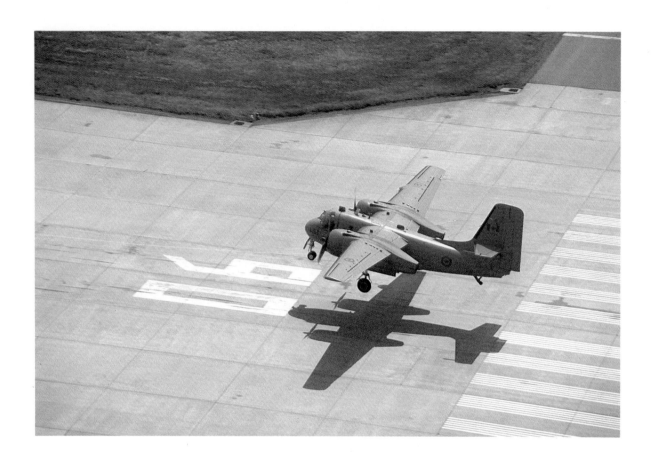

We also have a search and rescue (SAR) capability. Apart from assisting in searches we can fly top cover for Labrador helicopters, drop smoke and flares and serve as a radio relay for SAR aircraft operating on the deck. We can also drop a SKAD (survival kit air dropable) which contains inflatable rafts, rations and essential survival gear to see victims through until we can direct other SAR aircraft to the site. And we still fly a few sovereignty patrols (NORPATs) into the Arctic during the summer.

While our ASW role was removed way back in 1970, we're still capable of attacking lightly armed surface vessels with pods containing up to 36 air-to-surface CRV-7 rockets. They are completely unguided in that they fly straight out of the tubes in the direction the airplane is pointing when they are fired. But our more experienced pilots can consistently hit 45-gallon oil drums on the practice range. For a traditional "shot across the bow" statement they are more than adequate.

So I get to fly a beautiful old airplane with snarlin' radial engines – the last of a breed. It's great fun and they actually pay me to do it. I will miss her when she's gone.

A Tracker Pilot

SEA KING
CH-124

No pilot, on any of the 22 aircraft types in the Canadian Air Force inventory, will argue with the premise that flying the Sea King is one of the most demanding jobs in the military. Hovering 21,000 pounds of aircraft over a wildly pitching deck on the blackest night in the middle of the darkest ocean, on instruments alone, contributes to her reputation.

Pilots, like most people in the military, are looking for a challenge and I'm no exception. That's one of the reasons I wanted Sea Kings.

Besides flying the airplane, I like the mission. Providing a cordon of anti-submarine protection around surface ships in the fleet is what we're about and that's quite a responsibility for a crew of four. We're two pilots up front backed

up by a TACCO (tactical coordinator) and an AESOp (airborne electronic sensor operator). The TACCO is responsible for the tactical deployment of the Sea King, while the AESOp operates the dipping sonar transducer "ball" which he lowers into the water at the end of a 450-foot cable. It is an "active" sonar in that it sends out a ping which bounces back off the first thing it encounters. It will behave differently when it hits a submarine than it will when it hits the bottom or a tuna, and our AESOp interprets these returns. To use a top gun analogy, the AESOp hooks the submarine and the TACCO cleans and fries him. We also have Sonabuoys we can drop into the ocean with a preset depth. These are the "passive" listeners that tune in on sound emitted by the target submarine.

Our most potent deployment is the two ship packages aboard our Tribal Class destroyers. With two Sea Kings on the hunt a submarine will have a hard time shaking us, as one machine can be "dipping" while the other is moving closer to our best estimate of his position. By leapfrogging, with one of us always "listening" with our "ball" in the water, we rarely lose one. And once he's hooked we have a pair of Mk. 46 homing torpedoes to complete the process.

Our normal cruises are from three to six months and our HELAIRDETS (helo air detachments) on board consist of three crews for the two airplanes, plus 20 maintainers. The Sea King is one of the most complex machines currently flying with the Air Force and it requires about 23 man hours of maintenance for every flying hour. Our techs are top notch and they have earned our total respect and confidence for the enviable record of serviceability they maintain in cramped and difficult conditions.

anada has been at the forefront of ASW helicopter operations on an international scale and our HHRSD or helicopter haul-down rapid securing device is a prime example. This system allows us to land on a pitching deck under almost all weather conditions. While hovering over the deck, we lower a messenger wire and pull up a steel cable with which we actually secure the airborne aircraft to the centre of the deck. Our LSO (landing safety officer), himself a Sea King pilot, then applies tension to the cable from his position at the edge of the deck.

When he senses a stable platform he signals us to land. By keeping this tension, we can maintain a constant and safe distance from the rolling ship as we bring the aircraft on.

Another advantage is that as soon as the aircraft transitions from flying to being supported on deck, it's instantly attached to the ship. The "bear trap" box then closes on the probe extending from the belly of the Sea King and, with the tail secured, the LSO uses the bear trap to move the airplane along a groove in the deck into the hangar.

Another interesting feature of our Sea Kings is the hover trim control beside the back cargo door. At night, when the pilots up front have very little or no reference to maintain a hover, the AESOp can actually fly the airplane from the back door, and keep a stable hover over whatever we're working on. We also have the capability of refueling from the ship while in flight.

While our primary mission is ASW, we have a secondary responsibility for search and rescue, as well as a straight transport role. This means bringing supplies like food and mail aboard. I recall one two-day period when we brought 28,000 pounds of material to our ship with one bird.

I've been lucky to have had five tours on Sea Kings. After better than 4,000 hours flying them, it's still fun, still a very satisfying way to make a living.

A Sea King Pilot

AURORA
CP-140

Our Auroras provide Canada with the latest in high tech ASW capability. Our crews of ten consist of two pilots and a flight engineer up front with four navigators and three airborne electronic sensor operators (AESOp's) in the back. We're equipped with three on-board navigation systems that give us an all-weather, global capacity and the people in the back have all the latest in sophisticated electronic detection gear that allows us to find submarines.

To start with, we carry 96 Sonobuoys, devices we drop through tubes in the floor to preset depths where they "listen" for submarines. Then there's our magnetic anomaly detector (MAD) sticking out from the tail. It searches for anomalies in the earth's magnetic field generated by submarines. In addition we have radar and forward looking infrared (FLIR). A large central computer is used to collate and analyze all this data for us.

e carry only offensive weapons in the form of two types of homing torpedoes in our bomb bays, but the airplane is designed to allow us to quickly reconfigure for other weapons systems like the Harpoon air-to-surface missile. If we ever had to fight an airplane our only defence would be what they are now calling "evasive combat manoeuvring" (ECM).

At any rate, our environment would be low threat because our area of operations would be in the vicinity of the Canadian coast. As a result our most likely source of hostile fire would be limited to enemy submarines, and they would be tactically reluctant to engage us, since they would give away their position.

A good portion of our training is conducted with the U.S. Navy, utilizing their submarines as targets. The Soviets must have their own budget problems these days, because they're sending far fewer subs into our area of operations for us to play with.

Search and rescue, support for Department of Fisheries and Oceans and sovereignty patrols in the Arctic make up our secondary duties. Apart from showing the flag in the north on these NORPATS, we check and photograph abandoned airports, survival cairns, ice highways and bridges. With a range of 4,000 miles we can cover a lot of territory in a single flight.

For a pilot who wants to fly a large, highly sophisticated airplane, and get a lot of time doing it, the Aurora is the ship. Our crew days can easily go to 18 hours, with the average patrol lasting 10 hours, and so our pilots average 50 flying hours a month. They also get a lot of responsibility. We have pilots who are aircraft as well as crew commanders before their twenty-fifth birthdays.

With its four big GE T-56 turboprops turning out 5,000 shp, the airplane will do 400 kts, although our normal patrol speed is down around 200 kts. This allows us to conserve fuel and to maximize the performance of our detection equipment. And yet the Aurora flies like a jet with speeds similar to the Tutor. With its lighter control pressure it's a dream to manage, particularly compared to the old Argus.

They tell me I could retire this year, but I'm having too much fun.

An Aurora Pilot

THE MESS

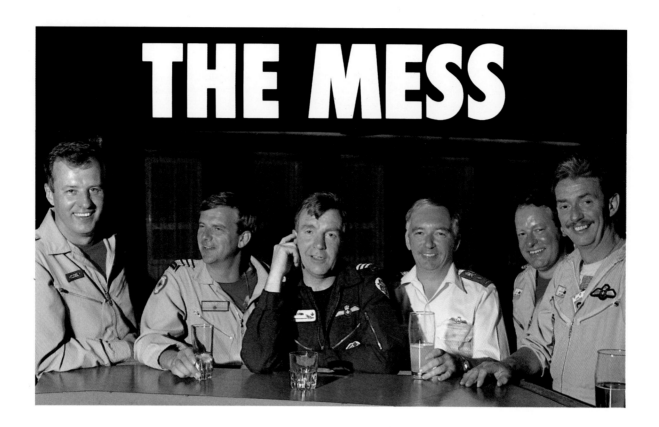

The mess is the oasis to which soldiers have retreated for centuries. Here they acquire a sort of immunity allowing for a more relaxed code of behaviour. Relaxed but with structure. What goes on in the mess stays in the mess. For this is truly a private club whose members all understand the code. And every mess observes the same rules, offers the same sanctuary. It is for members and invited guests only. It is a place to unwind and let off a little steam. It is a place where red tape can be cut or at least trimmed a little. It is a place where you are among friends.

Crud – a game played by Air Force people. It resembles snooker in the way that rugby resembles touch football.

FIGHTERS

Fighter Group is tasked with the defence of Canada against hostile intrusions of our airspace as part of our NORAD commitment. As a partner in NATO we also share the task of defending European airspace. Fighter Group in Canada has four squadrons dedicated (two each) to NORAD and NATO. Our three fighter squadrons devoted to the NATO role in Europe are part of 1 Canadian Air Division.

SILVER STAR T-33

CT-133

T-Birds have had a long and distinguished history with the Canadian Air Force. After serving for many years as a primary jet trainer they went on to perform in a variety of roles. Reluctant to completely shed their instructional mission, they found work towing targets for aerial and naval gunnery practice. They are also used as missile simulators. Flown against ships at 400 kts only a few feet off the waves, they are just like the Exocet coming at you and they provide realistic training for the Navy.

We also use them to calibrate our radar installations at Canadian Forces airports. As utility transport for parts and personnel they continue to give yeomen service, all the while supporting the biggest flying club in the Air Force.

We call her the "Humbler" in honour of her tendency to keep us all honest. You can always tell when a guy's not current on T-Birds because with that play in the stick on the roll axis he will be waving good-bye on climb out. Nothing fancy on the instrument panel. Just a regular old "stick and ball" airplane with standard flight and engine instruments, an ADF, Tacan, one UHF radio, plus guard. And a big old Rolls-Royce jet engine back there that's been doing just fine, thank you, since the early fifties.

Each time I climb into a T-Bird I haven't flown I check the little plate that tells when she was built. I found one that was just four months younger than I am.

A T-33 Pilot

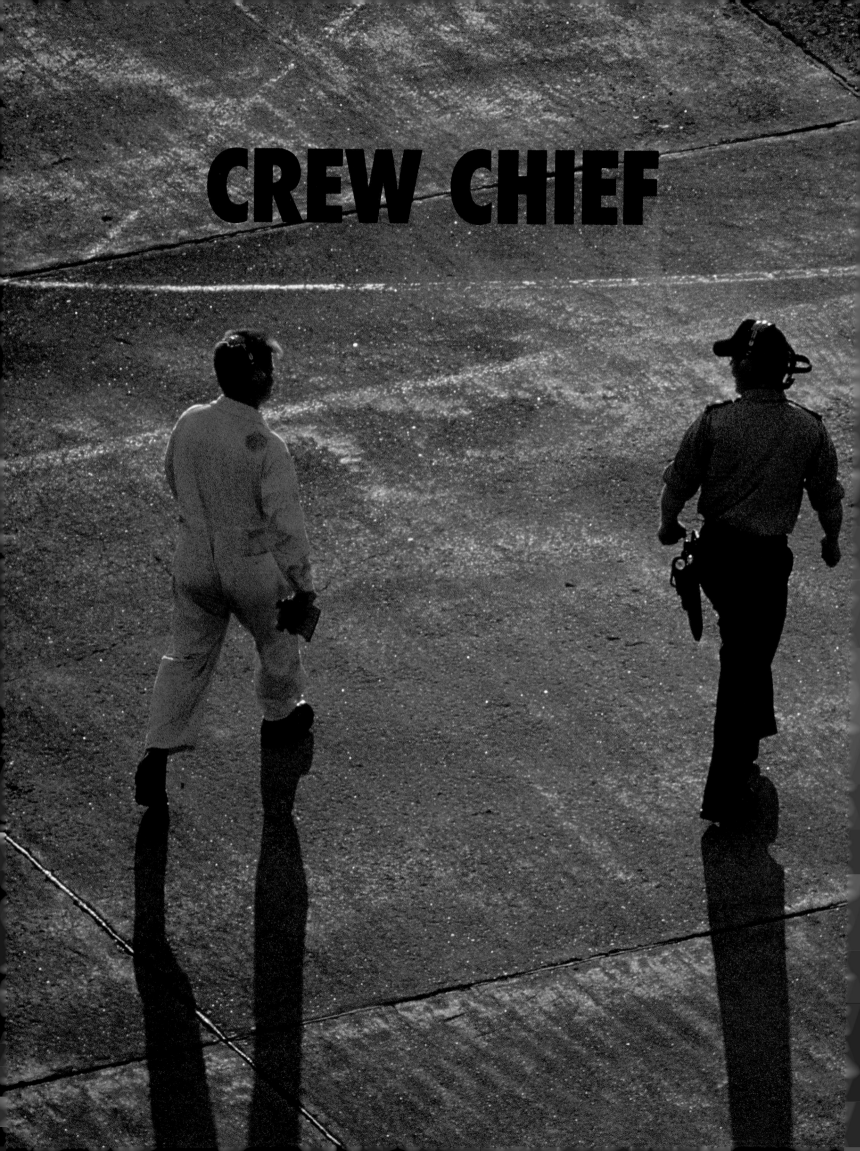

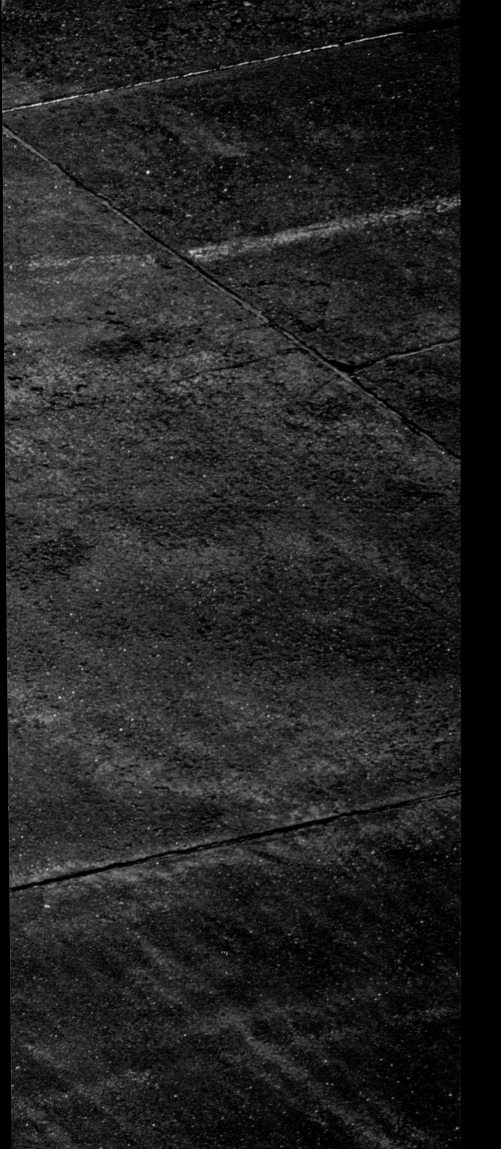

As crew chief I am responsible for all the technicians on my shift. We're "ops servicing," which means the line work from the servicing desk is our responsibility. Line servicing is what we call "first line maintenance." We pre-flight all squadron and transient aircraft (B checks), check them at the end of the day (A checks), and do turn-around inspections (AB checks). We also manage the start and park crews for out-bound and inbound airplanes. Pilots will report anything wrong with their aircraft to us and we pass it along to the snag desk if it's something we can't look after quickly, right out on the line. When the aircraft has to be hangared to be worked on we say it is in "second line mainten-ance." I am responsible for keeping the servicing board up to date. Each squadron aircraft is on this board and anyone looking at it should be able to tell, at a glance, the status of our machines at any given time.

On most bases we run two regular eight-hour shifts. The day chief personally briefs the night guy before going home. But at night you have to write it all in the "night book" because it will be eight hours before the day shift comes in.

The first thing I do in the morning is see how many "love letters" are waiting for me in those pages so I know what kind of day my crew can expect. Then I check the board, and with this information I can answer the question I get asked most often: "How many airplanes can you give me this morning Warrant?"

H ere at North Bay we have 24 men
and women on each of three line
crews, so that's a fairly large group
to manage. The Aurora crews at Green-
wood have almost 100, so it can get to
be quite a load. There's a lot of paper-
work, a reasonable share of frustration
and heartache, but there is a more than
reasonable level of job satisfaction. This
comes from working with great people
and keeping our Challengers and
T-Birds flying safely.

A Crew Chief

FREEDOM FIGHTER

CF-5

The business of piloting fighters begins here at Cold Lake. We use the CF-5 as a lead-in trainer for the CF-18. The school runs two seven-month courses a year and we usually graduate about 20 people per course. From here they cross over to the other side of the airfield where they strap on the Hornet and begin the advanced phase of fighter training.

The average group will be about 60 per cent new pilots fresh from Tutors at Moose Jaw with the remainder coming from other branches of the Air Force. We spend the first three months on basic conversion, teaching them to fly the F-5, while the last four are devoted to teaching them to actually fight the airplane.

The first phase focuses on learning the aircraft's systems, and then it's on to clear hood, instruments, aerobatics, formation flying and low-level navigation. The CF-5 is a pretty basic little airplane. That means no fancy radar or terrain avoidance gear so jettin' along 250 feet off the deck at 450 kts with a map on your knee makes for a little added intensity in the cockpit. On these trips the only instrument that will keep me and my student from ending up in the bottom of a smoking hole is the "Mark I Eyeball."

The second phase, employing the airplane as a weapons-delivery platform, is where the fun really starts. We teach air to ground using 20mm guns, CRV-7 rockets and iron bombs, and air-to-air with guns and heat-seeking missiles. In the air-to-air environment, a student's first six trips are BFM (basic fighter manoeuvring). And then he goes on to what he has spent the last two years of his life preparing for – ACM (air combat manoeuvring). He will begin with what we call "1-V-1 neutral" which means he will fly beak to beak, one versus one, against an instructor pilot (IP). When they pass each other the IP will call, "Fight's on" and they'll crank and bank for position. In this way neither of the pilots has any angle or energy advantage over the other at the merge, the point at which they actually pass each other and begin the engagement. So they're at opposing headings but the same altitude and airspeed. This will be followed by the more complex 1-V-2 and 2-V-1 offensive and defensive fights

All this activity takes place over a 7200-square-mile piece of real estate known as the Cold Lake Air Weapons Range. Part of this area is wired up with sensors that form the Air Combat Manoeuvring Range Instrumentation. The ACMRI enables the combatants to relive their engagement on a giant video screen and it's the most valuable training aid I've ever seen. With it there is no longer any of the "I got you – no I got you" stuff. It records all the moves and all the shots exactly as they occurred, for all to gloat or grimace over.

One thing I've noticed over the years is the dramatic change in the type of students we're getting in the Air Force today. In the old days fighter pilots tended to be younger, single and a little on the cowboy side of the maturity curve. Back in 1955 we lost over 100 F-86 Sabre pilots killed in that one year.

Join a group of students here today in the mess and you would probably find that, if they were not talking flying, they're more likely to be talking mortgage rates or their picks on the stock market than recounting escapades with the fairer sex. You would also discover all their past endeavours, and have experienced very little failure in their lives. They all seem to have a very positive, straight-ahead way of doing things.

One thing hasn't changed though. They might be a little more mature today, a little more educated, but – underneath it all – with 450 kts indicated and jet fuel exploding into noise behind them, that sophistication evaporates into balls-to-the-wall aggressiveness and you're looking at one formidable individual totally committed to mastering the skills necessary to piloting a jet fighter.

A Fighter Pilot Instructor, CF-5

IROQUOIS
CH-118

A "one bell" emergency means an aircraft from this base is down. Within five minutes I will be airborne in one of our single Huey helicopters with another pilot, a flight engineer, a doctor, a medaid and a firefighter. We call it "holding standby."

As a base rescue pilot this is my primary duty and it has a lot in common with our fighter pilots' responsibilities associated with "holding 'Q' " in Goose Bay or Comox. The nine bright yellow Hueys of Fighter Group assigned, three each, to Cold Lake, Bagotville and Goose Bay hold "five-minute standby" throughout the entire period of normal airport operations.

When regularly scheduled flying shuts down for the day our standby crew goes to a 30-minute alert status which means carrying the ever-present pager and sticking pretty close to the hangar. During our off-duty time we are on 8-hour recall for tasking from civilian agencies, search and rescue or medivac missions.

Our secondary duty is basic utility flying which means moving people and material around the base and out to the air weapons range.

One of the things I look forward to is the annual air show here at Cold Lake. We developed our own "Superman act" and I'm sure we get as much applause from the crowd when we take it on stage as the Hornet demo pilot inspires. The finale has our fully decked out Superman, feet firmly planted on the grass in front of the crowd, holding a mightily straining bright yellow Huey at the end of a 200 foot line over his head. Try as it might, the airborne helicopter can not overcome our hero's strength and it is eventually pulled down to earth. The kids, young and old, eat it up.

A Huey Pilot–Base Rescue

HORNET
CF-18

t was my first air show. I was 12 years old. The Voodoo pilot bewitched me with his routine of loops and rolls before disappearing in an ear-shattering vertical. In the silence he left behind, one dizzy young heart had been captured.

Air Cadets, a flying scholarship, private pilot's license before a driver's license, good grades because they said that was important – everything was focused on achieving that dream. To be a fighter pilot . . .

But what do you do when reality exceeds your dreams? Every time that canopy hums down and thunks closed, you know that is just what's going to happen.

With one movement of my left hand I can select full military power and send my body, and the 35,000 pounds of fire breathing airplane it is strapped into, hurtling through space faster than a 45 calibre bullet. Through the detents for afterburners or "light the pipes" and we are supersonic, leaving our own sound behind.

Just flying the airplane from A to B is easy. The CF-18 is a fly-by-wire aircraft, which means that flight control information is transmitted electronically from the stick to central computers. These computers then combine the pilot's input with data gleaned from several external sensors on the aircraft's skin. The hydraulic servos, which move the large control surfaces, are driven from these computers and are not linked directly to the stick as in most aircraft flying today. In auto flap mode the computer actually changes the shape of the wing's airfoil at different speeds and angles of attack to maximize performance. But flying the airplane sedately along is not what we're about. We are on the sharp end.

The CF-18 is a classic turn-and-burn, weapons delivery platform. It's the fighter pilot's job to employ these weapons. Air combat manoeuvring (ACM) or dog fighting is what drives us.

In the Canadian Air Force a fighter pilot has two distinct roles. In our NORAD role we are tasked with the defence of North American airspace against hostile intrusions. Fighters from our bases in Cold Lake, Bagotville, Comox and Goose Bay routinely intercept Russian bombers and escort them through our airspace.

It's a gentlemanly game where each team knows the rules, knows how far to push and takes care never to exceed the set limits. Our training simulates these types of threat responses.

In our fighter-intercept role we carry AIM-7M radar-guided Sparrow missiles, AIM-9M heat-seeking Sidewinder missiles, and a 20mm cannon. The Sidewinder's nose is so sensitive that it will send a hum into my headset when it picks up the heat from the exhaust of another ship on the flight line. When I hear it I'm always reminded of the low growl of a guard dog when it senses an unidentified presence in its space.

I n Europe our NATO squadron in Baden trains in an attack role, in keeping with our NATO commitment. If hostilities were to break out we would fly CAP (combat air patrols) over pre-assigned sectors operating in a defensive role until events either cooled down or escalated. If the cork really popped we would switch to the offensive. It's here that the Hornet really excels.

alk to anyone who operates F-18's and you'll be sure to hear about "big R and little M." They are referring to the jet's incredible record of high reliability and low maintenance. Last year we flew six machines from Alaska to the William Tell Competition in Florida and followed up with two weeks of hard flying without requiring one spare part. No doubt about it, we made the right choice.

A CF 18 Pilot

TECH

The CF-18 is the most technologically complex aircraft in the Air Force and Bagotville is an operational base in that same organization, so right here on this line is what they call the pointy end.

t's not for everyone. There's a lot of pressure to keep the jets launching, a lot more hours in the average workweek – what is called overtime in the civilian world – but I am just where I want to be. On this airplane we have armour, avionics systems, com radar, integral systems and engine and airframe specialists that all have to work together to keep our squadron's 12 Hornets flying. But everyone enjoys the satisfaction that comes from meeting those launch commitments. And the pilots express their appreciation directly to us, which makes a big difference. When I put my rank/first/last on the line saying my part of that airplane will fly, it's a good feeling because I know that

when the pilot signs that jet out, first he checks to make sure my signature's there.

A lot of times it feels like we all have two spouses. The person we walked down the aisle with and the Air Force – and often there's a suggestion that it is not necessarily in that order. But then there are all the opportunities for travel here in Europe plus the great social life on base. At Christmas there is the tradition we call 'Snowball' where everyone makes the rounds of friends' homes and it all sort of balances out in the end. I guess the way you see the world depends entirely on how you look at it.

An Aeroengine Tech CF-18

185

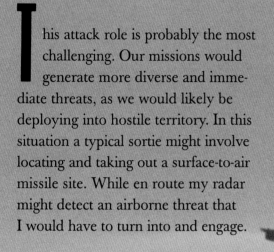

This attack role is probably the most challenging. Our missions would generate more diverse and immediate threats, as we would likely be deploying into hostile territory. In this situation a typical sortie might involve locating and taking out a surface-to-air missile site. While en route my radar might detect an airborne threat that I would have to turn into and engage.

Without taking my hand off the stick I can switch from ground attack to fighter mode, engage, and then shoot. I then switch back to ground attack, proceed to the target area, deliver my air-to-ground mud movers and leave. Our CF-18's are capable of carrying up to 17,000 pounds of ordinance, and below 13,000 pounds we can operate throughout our full 7.5g flight envelope. Not bad.

One really interesting innovation on our Canadian Hornets is the "false canopy" painted on the belly of the jet. It is intended to moment-arily confuse an enemy as to whether he is looking at the top or the bottom of our fighter. In ACM such confusion, no matter how fleeting, can turn a potential defeat into a victory. Not bad for a couple of bucks worth of paint.

For me, the most appealing part of being a fighter pilot is that we use both our analytical and intuitive capabilities in concert. Early fighter pilots relied entirely on their eyesight and their intuition to locate and engage an enemy, but radar and the missile age have changed all that.

In the CF-18 we have at least 14 different models of radar to assist us in detecting both airborne and ground-based threats. We have to be able to select and moni-tor the appropriate systems while we keep track of our fuel, our speed, where we are in space, where our friends are, and where the enemy is, or is likely to attack us from. We have to continually digest all this information while still flying the airplane. All this is what is called situational awareness.

And while yes, we have missiles, radar and jet engines – a roll is still a roll and a loop is still a loop. We still have a gun on the airplane to fire on an enemy who is inside the minimum range of our missiles and, like all fighter pilots before us, we still have those little hairs on the back of our necks.

So we have the speed and complexity of the information being presented to us combined with the speed at which we are travelling through space. These work together to make the cockpit of a modern jet fighter one of the most demanding office places in the world.

And then there are the G forces. Fighter pilots in World War II routinely pulled 5 or 6 G's but in their airplanes the

build-up was a little slower so they could lighten up on the stick when their vision started to tunnel and in this way avoid the more serious aspects of G-induced loss of control.

Put the CF-18 into a hard bat turn, however, and you can deal yourself a 7 or 8-G load instantly. This can mean a correspondingly instantaneous G-induced loss of consciousness with no advance warning. What happens then, is that you literally take a nap. The airplane itself takes over the flying, stops the turn for you and settles down into a nice straight and level one G straf target. Your opponent locks on, and you have a fighter pilot's "bad day" as he guns your brains out.

But being out there on the edge is where we want to be. The CF-18 is a single-pilot airplane. I am the pilot in command. While I alone employ the weapons, navigate and fly the aircraft, I have the support of hundreds of talented and highly dedicated human beings who work together to make it happen. It has to be the best job in the world.

A CF-18 Pilot

OPEN SKIES

As we go forward into the nineties changes on the international scene are happening faster than we can digest them. A few short years ago nobody would have believed a Soviet MiG 29 would be peacefully transiting the Canadian Rockies with a Canadian Hornet as his wingman.

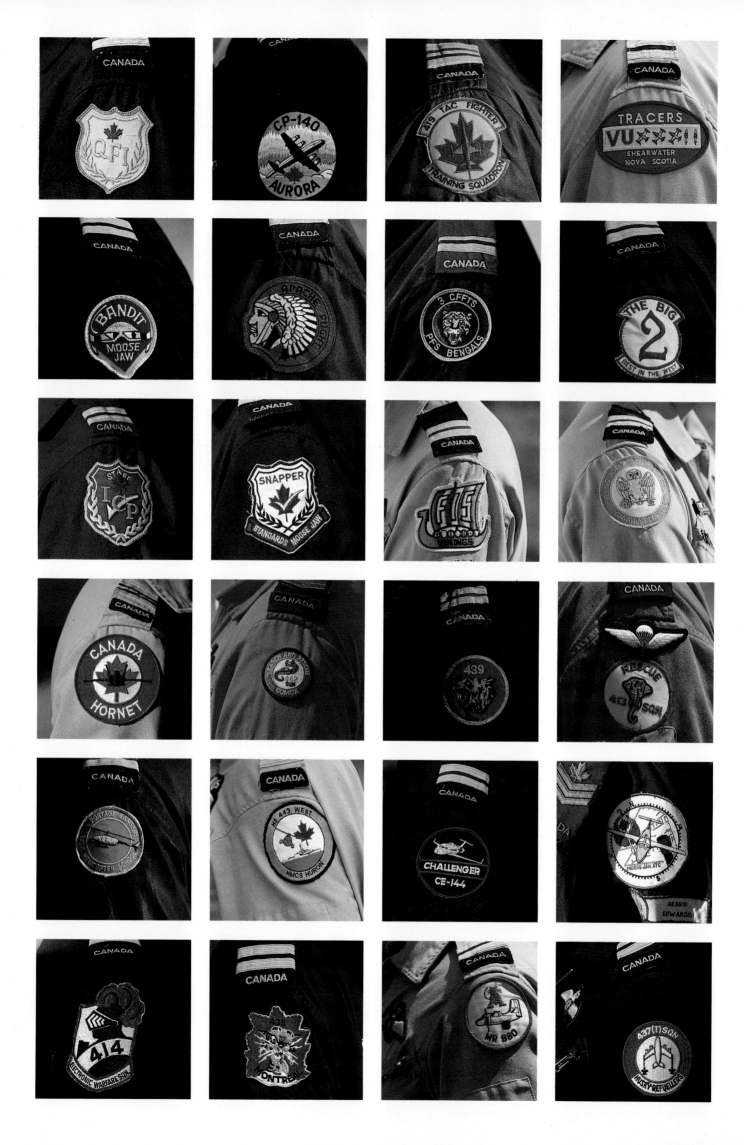

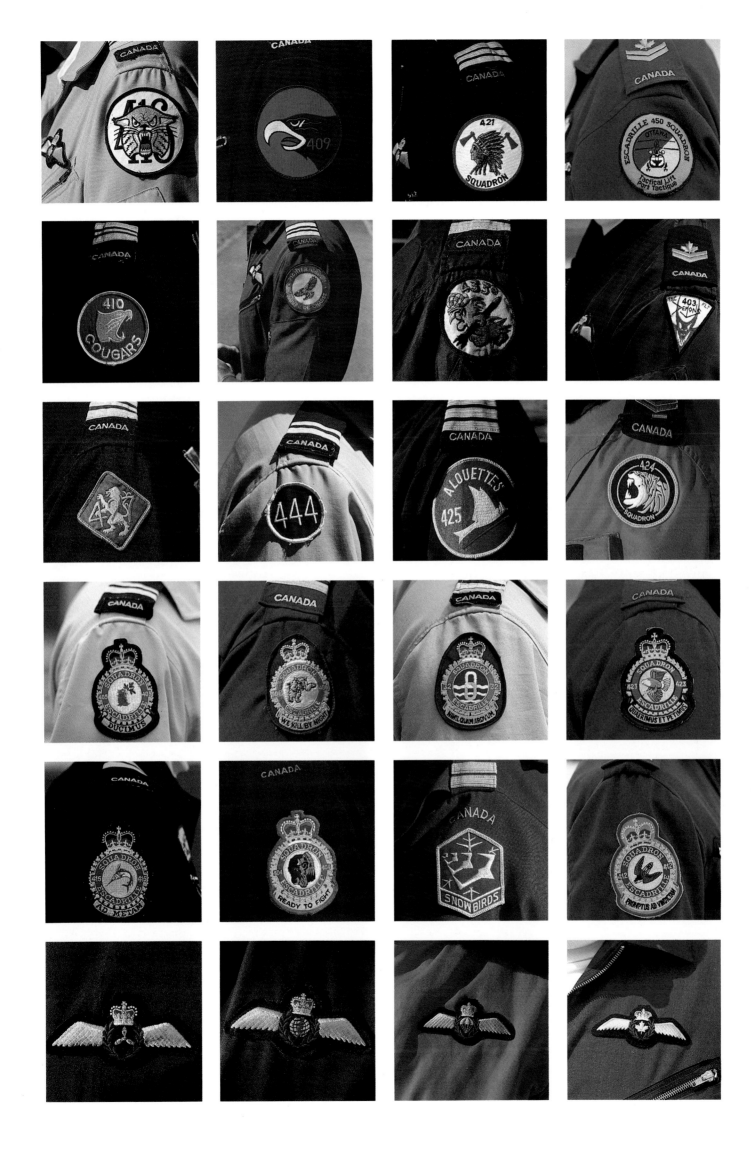

SPECS

MUSKETEER
CT-134

Prime Contractor: Beech
Length: 7.87 meters
Span: 9.98 meters
Weight: Basic 709 kg
Max 1,113.6 kg
Speed: 152 knots

Max Cruise: 133 knots
Normal Cruise: 105 knots
Power: One 180 hp Lycoming engine
Ceiling: 10,000 feet
Range: 700 nautical miles

JET RANGER
CH-139

Prime Contractor: Bell
Length: 9.50 meters
Rotor: 10.16 meters diameter
Max Weight: 1,460 kg
Speed: 130 mph (cruise)
140 mph (max)

Power: One Allison turboshaft
Endurance: 3 hours
Ceiling: 10,000 feet
Payload: 454 kg – 4 passengers plus pilot

TUTOR
CT-114

Prime Contractor: Canadair
Length: 9.75 meters
Span: 11.13 meters
Max Weight: 3,370 kg

Max Speed: 412 Knots
Power: General Electric J85-CAN-40 turbo-jet
Ceiling: 39,500 feet

TWIN HUEY
CH-135

Prime Contractor: Bell
Length: 17.45 meters
Rotor: 14.6 meters diameter
Weight: 2,865 kg (empty)
Speed: 130 knots (cruise)

Power: Two Pratt & Whitney (Canada) PT-6T turboshaft engines (United Aircraft Canada PT-6-T400)
Range: 250 nautical miles
Ceiling: 15,000 feet
Payload: 1,360 kg or 12 troops

CHINOOK
CH-147

Prime Contractor: Boeing
Length: 30 meters rotor tip-rotor tip
Rotor: 18.29 meters diameter
Speed: 155 mph (cruise)
202 mph (max)

Power: 6,600 shaft horse power maximum continuous to 7,830 shaft horse power for a maximum of 10 minutes
Range: 1,000 nautical miles (ferry)
Ceiling: 15,000 feet
Payload: 9,000 kg (or 42 combat-equipped troops or 24 casualty litters

KIOWA
CH-136

Prime Contractor: Bell
Length: 12.50 meters
Rotor: 10.75 meters diameter
Weight: 815 kg
Speed: 115 mph (cruise)
110 mph (max)
Power: One 317 shaft horse power turboshaft engine
Range: 230 miles plus 15-minute fuel reserve
Ceiling: 10,000 feet
Payload: 225 kg (excluding crew and fuel
Armament: One 7.62 mm Minigun/ or 2.75-inch Rockets

HERCULES
C-130

Prime Contractor: Lockheed
Length: 29.79 meters
Span: 40.41 meters
Max Weight: 70,000 kg max
Speed: 300 knots (cruise)
Power: Four Allison T-54-A-7/15 engines
Range: 2,700 miles (with 11,354 kg payload)
Ceiling: 35,000 feet
Max Payload: 20,454 kg

BUFFALO
CC-115

Prime Contractor: deHavilland
Length: 24 meters
Span: 29.25 meters
Weight: 18,600 kg
Speed: 260 mph (cruise)
Power: Two General Electric CT64-820-3 turbine engines
Payload: 41 fully equipped troops or equipment
Range: 1,400 miles

LABRADOR
CH-113

Prime Contractor: Boeing
Length: 25.40 meters
Max Weight: 9,707 meters
Normal Weight: 8,618 kg
Rotor: 15.24 meters diameter
Speed: 125 knots (cruise)
148 knots (max)
Power: Two T-58-GE-8F turbine engines
Range: 690 miles
Ceiling: 10,600 feet

TWIN OTTER
CC-138

Prime Contractor: deHavilland
Length: 15.77 meters
Span: 19.81 meters
Weight: 5,600 kg max
Speed: 180 mph (max)
170 mph (cruise)
Power: Two Pratt & Whitney Aircraft of Canada Limited PT6A-27 turboprop engines
Payload: 20 passengers or 2,000 kg cargo
Range: 900 nautical miles

DASH 8
CC-142

Prime Contractor: deHavilland
Length: 22.25 meters
Span: 25.60 meters
All-up Weight: 15,740 kg
Speed: 310 mph (max)
Power: Two Pratt & Whitney Aircraft of Canada Limited PW120A turbo-prop engines
Ceiling: 25,000 feet
Range: 575 miles

BOEING 707
CC-137

Prime Contractor: Boeing
Span: 44.19 meters
Length: 46.61 meters
Maximum Weight: 150,590 kg
Max Payload: 43,000 kg

Max Speed: Mach .81 (cruise)
Payload: 170 passengers plus 6,500 kg freight
Range: 6,000 miles
Ceiling: 42,000 feet

CHALLENGER
CC-144

Prime Contractor: Canadair
Length: 20.85 meters
Wingspan: 18.84 meters
Max Cruise Speed: Mach .80
Economical Cruise Speed: Mach .70
Ceiling: 41,000 feet

Power: A Model: Two AVCO Lycoming ALF 502L-2C engines B Model: Two General Electric CF34-1A turbofan engines
Payload: Four crew plus twelve passengers
Ferry Range: A Model: 2,500 Nautical miles B Model: 3,000 Nautical miles

COSMOPOLITAN
CC-109

Prime Contractor: Convair
Length: 24.84 meters
Span: 32.12 meters
Weight: 25,900 kg
Speed: 325 mph

Power: Two Allison 501-D36
Ceiling: 23,000 feet
Range: 2,000 nautical miles
Payload: 35 passengers

DAKOTA
CC-129

Prime Contractor: Douglas
Length: 20 meters
Span: 29 meters
Max Weight: 13,154 kg

Speed: 204 mph max
Power: Two Pratt and Whitney R-1830
Range: 505 miles
Ceiling: 10,000 feet

TRACKER
CP-121

Prime Contractor: deHavilland/Grumman
Length: 13 meters
Span: 23 meters
Weight: 11,818 kg (max)
Speed: 140 knots (search) 224 knots (max)

Power: Two Wright 983C9HEI nine-cylinder radial
Crew: 3
Range: 1,000 nautical miles
Ceiling: 24,000 feet
Armament: 2.75-inch rockets depth bombs bombs

SEA KING
CH-124

Prime Contractor: Sikorsky
Length: 16.69 meters
Width: 4.98 meters
Weight: 8,680 kg
Speed: 120 Knots (cruise) 144 Knots (max)

Power: 2 General Electric T-58-GE-8D Turbines
Ceiling: 10,000 feet
ASW Endurance: 3.5 hours or 400 miles
Armament: Homing torpedoes and depth bombs

AURORA
CP-140

Prime Contractor: Lockheed
Length: 35.37 meters
Wing Span: 30.37 meters
Max Gross Weight: 64,410 kg
Max Speed: 405 knots

Max Endurance: 17.7 hours
Ferry Range: 5,000 nautical miles
Ceiling: 35,000 feet
Crew: 10
Armament: Torpedoes

SILVER STAR T-33
CT-133

Prime Contractor: Lockheed
Length: 12 meters
Span: 14 meters
Max Weight: 7,636 kg

Speed: 450 mph (cruise)
550 plus (max)
Power: One Rolls-Royce Nene engine
Ceiling: 41,000 feet
Range: 1,250 miles (max)

FREEDOM FIGHTER
CF-5

Prime Contractor: Canadair/Northrop
Length: 14.38 meters
Span: 7.87 meters
Weight: Basic: 4,227 to 4,409 kg
Max: 9,090 kg
Speed: Mach 1.3

Power: TWO J85-CAN-15
Range: 500 to 1,000 nautical miles depending on configuration
Ceiling: 45,000 feet
Armament: Bombs-Rockets
20 mm gun
AIM-9 missile

IROQUOIS
CH-118

Prime Contractor: Bell
Length: 17.40 meters
Rotor: 14.63 meters diameter
Weight: 4,363.5 kg max
Speed: 120 mph (cruise)
140 mph (max)

Power: One Lycoming T-53 turboshaft
Endurance: 2 hours 15 minutes
Ceiling: 10,000 feet
Payload: 13 personnel (including crew)

HORNET
CF-18

Prime Contractor: McDonnell Douglas
Length: 17.07 meters
Wingspan: 12.31 meters
Gross Weight (Fighter Escort): 16,863 kg
Engines: 2 General Electric F404

Armament: Sidewinder and Sparrow air-to-air missiles Conventional bombs Rockets M-61 20 mm cannon
Combat Ceiling: 50,000 feet
Combat Radius: 600 nautical miles
Ferry Range: 2,000 nautical miles
Max Speed: Mach 1.8